TikTok for
Boomers

Table of Contents

Chapter 1: Introduction to TikTok
Chapter 2: Getting Started with TikTok
Chapter 3: Creating Engaging TikTok Content
Chapter 4: Decoding the TikTok Algorithm
Chapter 5: Finding Your Niche on TikTok
Chapter 6: Building a Loyal TikTok Community
Chapter 7: Creating Engaging Content that Stands Out
Chapter 8: How to Monetize Your TikTok Content
Chapter 9: Advanced TikTok Strategies for Going Viral
Chapter 10: TikTok for Personal and Professional Growth
Chapter 11: Advanced Features and Analytics
Chapter 12: Common Challenges and Solutions
Chapter 13: TikTok Etiquette and Safety
Chapter 14: The Psychology of TikTok Attraction
Chapter 15: The Future of TikTok
Chapter 16: Revisiting Viral Videos and Suggestions
Chapter 17: Embrace Your TikTok Journey

Chapter 1: Introduction to TikTok

Okay boomer, so you're interested in TikTok. Whether you've decided to join the platform and are looking to hit the ground running, been on for a while and just want a better grasp of how it all works, just fancy a few tips on what will make your next video go viral, or the kids are doing it and you want to know what the heck they're up to, this unofficial guide for boomers will give you everything you need to succeed or get with the times.

What is TikTok?

TikTok is a social media platform designed around short, engaging videos, and its stated mission is to "inspire creativity and bring joy." Unlike traditional apps that focus on connecting users with their immediate social circle, TikTok's approach revolves around exposing users to endlessly tailored content through its For You Page (FYP).
Since its global launch, TikTok has grown to dominate the social media landscape, competing with giants like YouTube, Instagram, and Facebook. However, its unique mix of accessibility and viral content creation has carved out a niche where anyone, regardless of their technical expertise, can create compelling, professional-looking videos.
As much as you may have heard to the contrary, TikTok is not just for kids. Despite the heavy adoption of the platform by teens in particular as an entertainment and communication source, it wasn't made for kids to the exclusion of others at all; in fact it's widely used by people of all ages and the app encourages this. Most prominent creators are adults, and to be included in TikTok's Creator Fund (ie receive a share of revenue), one of the criteria is to be at least 18 years old. So indeed, to make the most of TikTok, you need to be an adult.

The Magic of the TikTok Algorithm

The heart of TikTok's success lies in its algorithm. Every time a user opens the app, the For You Page suggests videos based on their preferences, often determined by:
1. Watch Time: Videos you watch repeatedly or finish.
2. Interactions: Likes, shares, follows, and comments.
3. Search Activity: Keywords and hashtags you explore.
4. Geographic and Language Preferences: Content suited to your location.

For creators, understanding this algorithm is essential. Here's how it works:
- Short Watch Time Rewards: If a video grabs attention in the first few seconds, it's more likely to be promoted.
- Engagement Signals: The more likes, shares, and comments your content gets, the more the algorithm promotes it.
- Freshness Matters: TikTok favors newly uploaded content over older videos.

Example:
A video featuring a person dancing to a trending song like "Cupid" by Fifty Fifty might initially be shown to 500 users. If 80% of these viewers engage (watching till the end, liking, or sharing), TikTok will expose the video to thousands, if not millions, of new users.

Why TikTok Matters for Adults

Adults increasingly use TikTok for reasons ranging from casual entertainment to professional development. Unlike the early perception of the app as a haven for teenage dance videos, today's TikTok offers:
1. Education: Learn skills through bite-sized tutorials.
2. Entertainment: Access creative content from diverse creators.
3. Networking: Discover and engage with like-minded individuals.
4. Self-Expression: Develop personal or brand identity.

TikTok provides an equal platform for creators. Whether you're 18 or 80, videos are judged on their creativity, not credentials.

A Cultural Force

TikTok's influence transcends the digital world. It has launched global trends, made everyday individuals famous, and significantly impacted industries like music and fashion.

Real-World Example:
The song "Old Town Road" by Lil Nas X was largely propelled to stardom by TikTok, where users created millions of videos featuring the song. It went on to break records, sitting at number one on the Billboard Hot 100 for 19 weeks.

TikTok has even influenced political movements, with users banding together to raise awareness, fundraise, and even prank public events.

Key Features

1. User-Friendly Video Editing: Built-in tools like filters, sound integration, and transitions make video creation accessible.
2. Trend Tracking: Explore trending hashtags and audio clips to stay relevant.
3. Collaboration Options:
    - Duets: Respond to another user's video side-by-side.
    - Stitch: Integrate another user's video clip into your own content.
4. Interactive Effects: From green screen tools to augmented reality filters.

TikTok Vocabulary

Before diving deeper, let's decode the TikTok lexicon:
- FYP: The For You Page, where curated content is displayed.
- Duet/Stitch: Features enabling video collaborations.
- Trending Sounds: Popular audio clips that help videos gain traction.
- Hashtag Challenges: Campaigns encouraging users to create themed videos, like #FlipTheSwitch.

TikTok Myths Debunked
1. "It's Just for Teens": False. Adults and professionals dominate niches like finance, wellness, and DIY.
2. "You Need Expensive Gear": False. Many viral videos are shot on smartphones.
3. "It's Hard to Get Noticed": False. TikTok's algorithm ensures even new users can go viral.

Chapter 2: Getting Started with TikTok

Why Setting Up Your Profile Matters
Your TikTok profile is your digital calling card. It's the first impression you make on viewers who explore your content. A thoughtfully crafted profile conveys credibility, creativity, and purpose. This chapter guides you through the essential steps to set up a professional, engaging, and discoverable TikTok profile.

Step 1: Downloading the App and Signing Up
1. Download the App: TikTok is available on iOS and Android devices. Search for "TikTok" in your app store, download, and install. Although you don't need the app to join and consume the platform (you can stay on your desktop or laptop if you like), the ability to engage fully with the TikTok community both as a viewer and as a creator is exponentially increased if you can engage at a moment's notice via your mobile device, wherever you are.
2. Create an Account:
   - Sign up using your email, phone number, or third-party services like Google, Facebook, or Apple ID.
   - Choose a memorable and meaningful username. Ideally, it should reflect your brand or personal identity, such as @TheDIYDad or @FitnessGuruJane.

Step 2: Understanding the Home Interface
TikTok's interface may feel overwhelming at first, but familiarity comes quickly:
- For You Page (FYP): Where the algorithm curates videos tailored to your preferences.
- Following Tab: Displays videos from accounts you follow.
- Discover Page: A hub for trending hashtags, sounds, and creators.
- Profile Page: Where your uploaded videos, bio, and profile picture appear.

Step 3: Optimizing Your Profile
A polished profile attracts followers and establishes trust. Focus on:
1. Profile Picture or Video:
   - Use a clear, high-quality image or opt for a short looping video to showcase your personality.
   - Ensure the image is relevant to your niche (e.g., a chef might use a picture of them cooking).

2. Username and Display Name:
   - Keep it simple, memorable, and reflective of your niche.
   - Example: If your username is @CraftyCathy, your display name could be "Cathy's Craft Corner."

3. Bio:
   - Limit: 80 characters.
   - Use this space wisely to describe your niche and call-to-action (CTA).
   - Example: "Sharing budget-friendly recipes 🔍 Follow for weekly tips!"

4. Link and Social Integration:
   - Add a website link if eligible (available after meeting follower thresholds).
   - Connect your Instagram and YouTube accounts to cross-promote content.

Step 4: Exploring TikTok's Features
Before creating content, familiarize yourself with TikTok's creative toolkit:
1. Record Button: Start creating videos with a single tap.
2. Effects: Experiment with filters, transitions, and augmented reality tools.
3. Sounds:
   - Browse trending songs and audio clips.
   - Save favorites for future use.

4. Editing Tools:
   - Trim clips, adjust speeds, or apply filters directly in the app.

5. Drafts: Save incomplete videos to refine later.

Step 5: Content Strategy for Beginners
To thrive on TikTok, focus on clarity and consistency:
1. Pick a Niche:
   - Define your target audience (e.g., fitness, comedy, education).
   - Tailor content to their interests and challenges.

2. Start Small:
   - Post short, simple videos to practice using TikTok's tools.
   - Example: Record a 15-second clip with a trending sound.

3. Follow Trends:
   - Monitor trending hashtags and challenges for inspiration.
   - Example: Participate in the #DayInTheLife trend by filming snippets of your routine.

4. Engage With Others:
   - Like, comment, and follow creators in your niche.
   - Build rapport with your audience through replies and duets.

Example Profile Setup for a Hypothetical User
Profile Name: Jane's Green Living
Username: @EcoFriendlyJane
Profile Picture: A smiling Jane holding a plant.
Bio: "Easy eco-tips 🌍 DIY hacks for a greener home 🌱 Follow for weekly updates!"
Content Plan: Weekly uploads showcasing DIY eco-projects, plus participation in trending challenges.

Common Mistakes to Avoid
1. Unclear Branding: A generic username or bio can confuse potential followers. Make sure visitors to your profile get an accurate understanding of the persona or product that you're cultivating when choosing a name and accompanying images.
2. Inconsistent Posting: Irregular uploads hurt visibility. It helps to make posting a regular part of your activity if viewer engagement is a goal.
3. Ignoring Analytics: Track performance using TikTok's Pro Account insights to refine your strategy and stay on top of what works.

The Road Ahead
With your profile set up and an understanding of TikTok's tools, you're ready to create and share content. The next chapter dives into crafting engaging, high-quality videos that resonate with your audience.

Chapter 3: Creating Engaging TikTok Content

The Essence of Engagement
Creating content that engages viewers is at the heart of TikTok success. Engagement includes likes, comments, shares, and follows, and it indicates that your videos are resonating with your audience. This chapter will guide you through crafting videos that stand out and connect with your target audience.

1. Understanding TikTok's Content Formula
Engaging TikTok videos often follow a specific pattern:
1. Hook: The first 3 seconds are critical. Use surprising visuals, a bold statement, or a provocative question to grab attention.
   - Example: Start with, "You won't believe how easy this recipe is!"

2. Story or Value: Deliver the main content quickly and clearly. TikTok thrives on brevity; show, don't tell.
   - Example: Use captions or sped-up clips to demonstrate a cooking process.

3. Call to Action (CTA): Encourage viewers to engage, like, or follow.
   - Example: "Comment below with your favorite hack!"

2. Types of Content That Thrive on TikTok
Different types of videos succeed depending on your niche and audience. Popular categories include:
1. Tutorials and How-To Videos:
   - Short, informative clips providing value.
   - Example: A 15-second skincare hack or a one-minute DIY project.

2. Trends and Challenges:
   - Participate in trending challenges or use viral sounds.
   - Example: Joining a dance trend with your unique twist.

3. Storytime Videos:
   - Share compelling or humorous stories with captions for accessibility.
   - Example: "The time I accidentally ruined Thanksgiving dinner…"

4. Transformational Content:
   - Showcase before-and-after results.
   - Example: Fitness progress, home renovations, or art projects.

5. Relatable Humor:
   - Use memes and situational comedy.
   - Example: Create a skit about daily struggles, like forgetting your wallet at the store.

6. Behind-the-Scenes (BTS) Content:

- Offer a glimpse into your life or creative process.
- Example: A "day in the life" video for a content creator.

3. Harnessing TikTok's Creative Tools
TikTok provides built-in tools to enhance your videos. Experiment with these features:
1. Sounds and Music:
   - Music is integral to TikTok. Align your content with trending sounds.
   - Save popular audio clips to incorporate into future videos.

2. Effects:
   - Augmented reality filters, transitions, and interactive effects can elevate your content.
   - Example: Use green-screen effects to transport yourself to imaginary locations.

3. Text and Captions:
   - Overlay text to emphasize key points or create dialogue.
   - Example: Use bold fonts for humorous captions.

4. Editing Features:
   - Trim clips, adjust speeds, and add transitions for polished results.
   - Consider experimenting with jump cuts for dynamic pacing.

4. Storyboarding and Pre-Planning
Although TikTok videos are brief, planning your content ensures clarity and impact:
1. Outline Your Concept:
   - Decide on your video's goal (e.g., educate, entertain, inspire).
   - Plan key shots or scenes.

2. Script Writing:
   - Write concise scripts for complex videos to maintain focus.

3. Practice Makes Perfect:
   - Rehearse before filming - a tight performance makes good viewing.

5. Shooting Techniques for Eye-Catching Videos
1. Lighting:
   - Use natural light or affordable ring lights for professional-looking results.

2. Framing:
   - Align key subjects in the center of the frame.
   - Use TikTok's guidelines to position text overlays effectively.

3. Stabilization:
   - Use tripods or phone stabilizers for smooth footage.

6. Editing Like a Pro
Editing is where raw footage transforms into viral-worthy content:
1. Match Cuts:
   - TikTok will loop your video endlessly (and the longer, the better), so a seamless transition from the end back to the beginning is key to multiple plays. Focus particularly on beats in the music to form a pleasing loop wherever possible.

2. Pacing:
   - Keep the energy high with quick cuts and engaging transitions.

3. Experimentation:
   - Test different styles to discover what resonates with your audience.

7. Posting at the Right Time
Timing impacts visibility, so posting at the right time on TikTok is crucial for maximizing engagement, as it ensures your content reaches your audience when they're most active. While there isn't a universal "best time", you can optimize your posting schedule using several strategies:

1. **Understand Audience Activity Patterns**
   Analyze your audience's behavior through TikTok's built-in analytics. Navigate to the **Followers** tab in your account's analytics section to identify when your followers are most active by hour and day. This insight provides a tailored approach to posting times, especially for your specific audience demographics.

2. **General Best Times**
   Research suggests that posting earlier in the day often yields higher engagement, with weekdays at 10 a.m. PST being a common recommendation. Thursdays and Fridays also tend to have increased activity as users prepare for the weekend.

3. **Consider Time Zones**
   If your audience spans multiple regions or countries, time zones are vital. For instance, a post that performs well in Eastern Standard Time (EST) might need adjustment for audiences in Pacific Time (PST), or further adjustment for international views.

4. **Test and Monitor Performance**
   Experiment with posting at different times and days, then monitor how your content performs. Look at metrics such as likes, shares, and average watch time to fine-tune your schedule.

5. **Leverage External Tools**
   Platforms like Iconosquare and Later offer tools to help identify optimal posting times. These tools analyze engagement data over time to suggest the best windows for publishing your content.

By consistently refining your posting strategy and aligning it with your audience's habits, you can significantly boost the visibility and engagement of your TikTok videos.

8. Learning From Analytics
Your analytics can reveal what works and what doesn't:
1. Metrics to Monitor:
   - Views: Indicates reach.
   - Likes, Comments, and Shares: Reflect engagement.
   - Completion Rate: Tracks how many viewers watched the entire video.
   - Viewer demographics: Age brackets, gender, location

2. Refining Content:
   - Analyze high-performing videos to replicate successful elements.

Example: Crafting a Viral TikTok
Imagine a video about a DIY kitchen hack:
1. Start with a hook: "Stop throwing away your old mason jars!"
2. Showcase the hack: Quickly demonstrate how to repurpose jars into storage containers.
3. Add value: Include tips for labeling and organizing.
4. CTA: End with, "Follow for more kitchen hacks!"

Common Pitfalls to Avoid
1. Low-Quality Videos:
   - Poor lighting or sound can deter viewers.

2. Overcomplicating Content:
   - Simplicity is key. Avoid overwhelming viewers with excessive information.

3. Ignoring Trends:
   - Staying current with trends keeps your content relevant. Be a watcher, not just a creator.

The Next Step
With the ability to create engaging TikTok videos, you're ready to optimize your content for maximum visibility and growth. The next chapter will cover TikTok's mysterious algorithm and how to leverage it to your advantage.

Chapter 4: Decoding the TikTok Algorithm

Understanding the Algorithm
The TikTok algorithm is the secret sauce behind the platform's ability to deliver highly engaging and personalized content to users. It determines which videos appear on a user's For You Page (FYP), the primary driver of visibility and growth for creators.

1. How the Algorithm Works
TikTok's algorithm analyzes various signals to determine which videos to promote. These include:
1. User Interactions:
   - Engagements like likes, shares, comments, and follows signal interest.
   - Video completions are a critical metric. A high completion rate increases the likelihood of promotion.

2. Video Information:
   - Captions, hashtags, sounds, and effects inform the algorithm about the video's content and context.
   - Keywords in captions and text overlays can help categorize your content.

3. Device and Account Settings:
   - Location, language, and device type may influence which videos are shown but are less impactful than engagement signals.

4. Watch History:
   - The algorithm prioritizes content similar to what users have interacted with previously.

5. Diversity of Content:
   - TikTok mixes trending and niche content to keep users engaged.

2. Cracking the FYP Code
Getting your content on the FYP is a key to virality. Here's how to optimize for it:
1. Engage Early:
   - TikTok tests new videos with a small audience. Strong early engagement prompts the algorithm to push your video to a wider audience.
   - Encourage interaction with a call to action: "Double-tap if you agree!" or "Tag a friend who needs to see this!"

2. Optimize Video Length:
   - Shorter videos with high completion rates perform better. Aim for 15–30 seconds if possible, but longer content can succeed if it remains engaging throughout.

3. Leverage Trends:

- Use trending sounds, hashtags, and challenges while adding your unique twist.
- Example: If a dance trend is popular, incorporate it into your niche, such as a comedy or educational spin.

4. Engage With Comments:
   - Responding to comments on your video boosts engagement.
   - Use the "Reply with Video" feature to answer popular questions or engage directly with your audience.

3. Hashtags and Captions: The Unsung Heroes

Using the right hashtags and captions can significantly increase discoverability:

1. Hashtag Strategy:
   - Combine broad, trending hashtags (#FYP, #Viral, #Trending) with niche-specific ones (#FitnessTips, #DIYProjects).
   - Avoid overloading your video with hashtags; 3–5 relevant ones are sufficient.

2. Captions:
   - Write captions that intrigue or engage the viewer.
   - Example: Instead of "Look at this cake," say, "This cake looks normal, but wait until I cut into it…"

4. Timing Matters

While TikTok's algorithm promotes content over time, posting when your audience is active increases the likelihood of initial engagement. Use TikTok Analytics to determine when your followers are online and schedule posts accordingly.

5. Experimentation and Data-Driven Adjustments

1. A/B Testing:
   - Try different types of content, captions, and hashtags to see what works best.
   - Example: Post similar videos with slightly different captions and analyze performance.

2. Analyze Metrics:
   - Use TikTok's Analytics to understand what resonates with your audience.
   - Key Metrics:
     - Reach: How many people saw your video.
     - Engagement: Likes, comments, and shares.
     - Completion Rate: Percentage of viewers who watched the entire video.

6. Engaging With TikTok Trends

Staying relevant with trends is crucial for success:

1. Follow Trendsetters:
   - Observe how top creators in your niche use trends creatively.

2. Act Quickly:
   - Jump on trends as they emerge for maximum impact.

3. Blend Trends With Originality:
   - Avoid copying trends outright. Add a unique twist that aligns with your personal brand.

7. Avoiding Algorithm Pitfalls
1. Overloading With Hashtags:
   - Focus on relevance rather than quantity.

2. Inconsistent Posting:
   - Regular uploads signal the algorithm that you're an active creator.

3. Ignoring Video Quality:
   - Poor lighting or sound can detract from your content.

Example: A Viral TikTok Breakdown
Let's consider a viral video about making coffee art:
1. Hook: The video opens with a question: "Think you can't make latte art? Watch this!"
2. Content: The creator shows step-by-step how to create a heart shape with milk foam.
3. Engagement: They finish with a CTA: "Comment with your favorite coffee drink!"
4. Trend Use: The video features a popular sound tagged #LatteLove and #BaristaTips.

This formula ensures discoverability and engagement, aligning perfectly with TikTok's algorithm preferences.

8. Staying Flexible
TikTok's algorithm evolves over time. Staying adaptable and continuously learning ensures sustained success on the platform, so invest a little time now and then in researching its eccentricities and biases (ie a quick internet search on the current nature of the algorithm) to make sure you're up to date.

The Next Step
With a deeper understanding of TikTok's algorithm, you're ready to apply this knowledge to your content strategy. The next chapters will focus on finding a niche and building a loyal TikTok community, helping you convert viewers into dedicated followers.

Chapter 5: Finding Your Niche on TikTok

The Importance of Niche Content for Building a Loyal Audience

TikTok is an immense platform where millions of videos are uploaded every day, covering a vast array of topics. To stand out in this sea of content, it's essential to have a clear focus. This is where the concept of a "niche" comes in.

A niche is a specific subject or area of interest that you consistently create content about. By carving out a niche, you can attract a targeted, loyal audience who shares your interests. The importance of this is twofold: not only does it help you stand out, but it also builds a sense of community. Viewers who share your passion or interests will feel more connected to you, encouraging them to follow you and engage with your content.

In this chapter, we'll explore why having a niche is critical to success on TikTok, delve into examples of popular niches, and offer practical advice for finding and owning your niche.

Why Finding Your Niche Matters

1. Building a Loyal Audience

A clear niche allows you to target a specific group of people, which is key to growing your follower count. According to social media experts, when you focus your content on a specific topic, you're more likely to attract viewers who are genuinely interested in that topic, which leads to better engagement. This makes it easier to build a loyal audience who will keep coming back for more content.

The TikTok algorithm also rewards creators who maintain a focused approach, because it helps the app understand who to show your content to. If you consistently post content related to a specific niche, the algorithm will serve your videos to users who have engaged with similar content, boosting your chances of gaining more followers.

2. Establishing Your Expertise

When you consistently post about a particular subject, you start to establish yourself as an expert or thought leader in that field. People are more likely to follow someone who provides value, whether it's through entertainment, education, or inspiration. This expertise will build trust, making your followers more likely to engage with your content and share it with others.

3. Standing Out from the Crowd

While TikTok offers a wide variety of content, standing out is key. Generalist content can get lost in the crowd, while niche content targets people who are passionate about that specific topic. Whether it's a specialized form of humor, a unique hobby, or an emerging trend, finding your niche ensures you're not trying to appeal to everyone but to the right people.

Examples of Popular Niches on TikTok

TikTok covers an immense range of topics, and finding a niche that fits you can make all the difference in terms of success. Here are a few examples of popular niches that have cultivated large, dedicated followings:

1. Cooking and Food
The cooking and food niche is incredibly popular on TikTok, where creators post everything from recipes to food hacks to restaurant reviews. Channels dedicated to specialized food content, such as vegan meals, budget cooking, or international cuisines, have cultivated loyal followers eager to try new dishes or learn specific culinary skills.
Example: @cookingwithshereen – Shereen, a self-taught home cook, has built a huge following by sharing recipes that are simple, fun, and accessible to all levels of cooks.

2. Fitness and Health
Fitness is another booming niche, and TikTok is a great platform for fitness influencers to post workout routines, fitness challenges, and wellness advice. There are niches within the fitness category itself, such as strength training, yoga, or bodyweight exercises, catering to different audience interests.
Example: @kelsey_jn – Kelsey creates short and impactful workout videos for people looking to stay fit with quick routines, especially focused on beginners or those working with limited time.

3. Comedy and Humor
TikTok thrives on comedy content, from skits to memes to hilarious challenges. Those who specialize in making people laugh often find great success, as humor is one of the most shareable types of content. TikTok's short-form video format is perfect for comedic timing.
Example: @spencerx – Known for his musical talents and funny, exaggerated humor, SpencerX has built a loyal following through both his impressive beatboxing skills and comedic content.

4. Beauty and Fashion
The beauty and fashion niche is massive on TikTok. Creators in this area often focus on makeup tutorials, fashion tips, product reviews, or even sustainable fashion. As TikTok is such a visual platform, it's an ideal space to showcase creativity in these areas.
Example: @kaitlynnedwards – Kaitlyn shares daily outfits, makeup tutorials, and beauty hacks, often with a focus on budget-friendly or "thrifted" fashion options.

5. Pets and Animals
People love watching videos of adorable animals, and TikTok's algorithms favor content that gets high engagement. Many pet accounts, whether they feature specific pets or just funny animal videos, have gone viral thanks to their niche appeal.
Example: @itsdougthepug – Doug the Pug has amassed millions of followers by creating content around his adorable antics and engaging personality, showing the massive appeal of pets on TikTok.

Tips for Finding and Owning Your Niche

Now that we've discussed why finding a niche is so important and looked at some popular examples, let's break down how you can discover and commit to your own niche.

1. Explore Your Interests and Passions

Start by thinking about what excites you. TikTok is a platform that thrives on passion and creativity, so creating content about something you love will come more naturally. Ask yourself: What do I enjoy doing in my free time? What topics am I always talking about with friends? Do I have any unique skills, hobbies, or experiences that might resonate with others?

Your niche doesn't have to be something overly specific or obscure. It can be something broad that you can put your personal twist on. If you love cooking, maybe focus on budget-friendly meals or quick recipes for busy people.

2. Research Your Competitors

Take a look at what other creators in your chosen niche are doing. See what's working for them and what kind of content gets the most engagement. This will give you insight into what the audience likes and what's already being done. Don't try to copy exactly, but look for patterns that you can learn from.

3. Focus on What Makes You Unique

What can you offer that's different from other creators? Maybe it's a unique angle, a specific skill, or even your sense of humor. Finding your unique voice within a niche is what will help you stand out.

4. Experiment with Different Content Types

It's important to test a variety of content formats until you find the one that works best for you. Whether it's tutorials, challenges, live streams, or storytelling, try different approaches and see what resonates with your audience.

5. Don't Be Afraid to Evolve

Your niche doesn't have to be set in stone. As you grow and evolve as a creator, your interests may shift, and your audience may evolve with you. Don't be afraid to pivot or add new elements to your content as long as it still aligns with your brand.

Conclusion: Owning Your Niche and Growing Your Audience

TikTok thrives on unique and engaging content, and carving out a niche allows you to focus your creative energy on what you do best. By staying consistent, exploring your interests, and being authentic, you'll begin to build a dedicated audience that values the content you create.

Finding your niche on TikTok is not about pigeonholing yourself, but about narrowing your focus so you can stand out in a crowded space. Once you discover your niche and start creating with authenticity and passion, the possibilities for growth are endless.

By following these steps and examples, you'll be well on your way to not just finding a niche, but truly owning it, building a loyal following, and creating content that resonates with people who share your interests. Happy creating!

Chapter 6: Building a Loyal TikTok Community

Why Community Matters
On TikTok, success isn't just about creating viral content; it's about cultivating a loyal audience. A strong community ensures that your content gets consistent engagement, creates opportunities for collaboration, and allows for long-term growth. A loyal following can turn your TikTok presence into a personal brand or business.

1. Define Your Audience
The first step in building a community is knowing who you're speaking to:
1. Identify Your Niche:
   - Consider your passions, expertise, or unique experiences.
   - Examples: Fitness, parenting, cooking, humor, or tech reviews.

2. Know Your Audience's Interests:
   - Use TikTok's Analytics to understand the demographics and preferences of your audience.
   - What problems do they want to solve? What content entertains or informs them?

3. Align Your Content:
   - Create videos that resonate with your audience while staying authentic to your brand.

2. Engage Authentically
Engagement is a two-way street. Actively interacting with your audience fosters loyalty:
1. Respond to Comments:
   - Reply to comments on your videos to build rapport. Use humor, insights, or thoughtful replies.
   - Example: If someone compliments your recipe, reply with, "Thanks! What's your favorite dish to make?"

2. Live Streams:
   - TikTok Live allows real-time interaction. Use it to answer questions, share behind-the-scenes content, or host Q&A sessions.
   - Example: A travel creator could go live from a unique location, sharing tips and answering viewer questions.

3. Reply With Videos:
   - Use TikTok's "Reply with Video" feature to turn comments into content.
   - Example: If a viewer asks, "How did you learn this skill?" create a video detailing your journey.

3. Post Consistently
Consistency signals reliability to your audience and the TikTok algorithm. Develop a posting schedule that balances frequency and quality:
1. Determine Your Cadence:
   - Start with 3–5 posts per week and adjust based on your capacity and audience response.
2. Batch Content Creation:
   - Dedicate time to create multiple videos at once, for staggered posting. This ensures a steady stream of content even when life gets busy.
3. Use Analytics to Schedule:
   - Post during peak audience activity times as determined by your TikTok Analytics.

4. Encourage User Participation
User-generated content fosters a sense of community and extends your reach:
1. Challenges and Trends:
   - Create a unique hashtag challenge to encourage audience participation.
   - Example: A fitness creator could launch a #7DayPlankChallenge, inviting followers to join and share their progress.
2. Duets and Stitches:
   - Encourage your followers to duet or stitch your videos.
   - Example: A music creator could post a track snippet and invite followers to add vocals or instruments.
3. Feature Your Fans:
   - Highlight user-generated content on your page to show appreciation.

5. Collaborate With Other Creators
Partnering with creators in your niche expands your reach and enriches your community:
1. Find Compatible Creators:
   - Look for creators whose audience overlaps with yours but who bring a different perspective.
   - Example: A food blogger could collaborate with a fitness influencer to create healthy recipe content.
2. Collaborative Content Ideas:
   - Co-create videos, host joint live streams, or challenge each other to trends.

6. Provide Value
Your community will stick around if your content adds value to their lives:
1. Teach or Entertain:
   - Solve problems, share insights, or provide laughs (or combine for greater impact).

- Example: A parenting creator could share "5 Tips for Stress-Free Bedtime."

2. Be Relatable:
   - Share personal stories or challenges to humanize your content. We love seeing ourselves reflected in the experiences of others.

7. Create a Brand Identity
Strong branding helps your audience recognize and connect with your content:
1. Visual Consistency:
   - Use consistent colors, fonts, or effects in your videos.

2. Catchphrases or Themes:
   - Develop a signature catchphrase, sound, or style.

8. Foster a Positive Environment
1. Set the Tone:
   - Encourage positivity in your comments section and content.

2. Moderate Proactively:
   - Use TikTok's tools to filter offensive language and block disruptive users.

Example Study: A Community in Action
Let's look at an example of a creator and the engagement plan that built a thriving TikTok community:
- Creator: A DIY home improvement enthusiast.
- Strategy:
   1. Shared simple, beginner-friendly tutorials.
   2. Responded to followers' questions in the comments with video replies.
   3. Hosted live Q&A sessions to address project challenges.
   4. Encouraged followers to post their projects using the hashtag #DIYWith[Name].

Within months, their hashtag had thousands of contributions, and they built a loyal following eager to engage and learn.

9. Long-Term Engagement
Sustaining a community requires continuous effort:
1. Evolve With Your Audience:
   - Pay attention to trends and adapt to your audience's changing interests.

2. Appreciate Milestones:
   - Celebrate follower milestones with giveaways, special content, live events, or simple gratitude.

The Boomer Bottom Line
Building a TikTok community takes time, authenticity, and strategic effort. However, the rewards - a dedicated audience, increased visibility, and potential monetization opportunities - make the investment worthwhile.

Chapter 7: Creating Engaging Content that Stands Out

TikTok's lifeblood is its content. To succeed, your videos must not only grab attention but also keep viewers engaged long enough to interact and share. Creating standout content is about combining creativity with strategy, ensuring your videos resonate with viewers and the TikTok algorithm alike.

1. Understand What "Engaging" Means
Engaging content captures the viewer's attention, holds it, and motivates action - whether that's liking, commenting, sharing, or following. Metrics to aim for include:
- High Retention: Keep viewers watching until the end.
- Interactions: Encourage comments, shares, or duets.
- Replayability: Videos viewers want to rewatch.

2. Master the Art of the Hook
The first few seconds of your video are critical for capturing attention. A strong hook sets the stage:
1. Start With a Question or Statement:
   - Example: "Did you know this simple trick can save you hours?"

2. Show Something Unexpected:
   - A sudden action or striking image can immediately intrigue viewers.

3. Use Text Overlays:
   - Highlight the video's theme or purpose within the first 3 seconds.

3. Embrace TikTok Trends
Leveraging trends is essential for visibility and virality:
1. Participate Early:
   - Identify trending hashtags, sounds, or challenges on TikTok's Discover page.
   - Example: A creator might join a viral dance challenge but add a humorous twist to stand out.

2. Add a Personal Spin:
   - Stand out by customizing trends to align with your niche, by uploading a video that uses unique hashtags, catchy music, or a distinct format that invites participation. Engaging your followers and prompting them to replicate your trend (like with a hashtag challenge) can help you grow your presence and start a viral trend.

3. Follow Emerging Audio Trends:
   - Use TikTok's trending sounds to boost discoverability. Ensure the sound fits your video's theme.

4. Make Use of Storytelling

TikTok is perfect for micro-storytelling. Use its short-form format to craft compelling narratives:

1. Structure Your Story:
   - Beginning: Set up the context.
   - Middle: Build anticipation or introduce conflict.
   - End: Deliver a resolution, punchline, or surprise.

2. Incorporate Relatable Themes:
   - Stories about common experiences or emotions are universally appealing.
   - Example: A video about an embarrassing childhood moment might resonate broadly.

5. Enhance with Visual Appeal

TikTok is a visually driven platform. Even simple ideas can shine with the right visuals:

1. Use High-Quality Video:
   - Ensure your videos are clear and well-lit.
   - Use natural light or ring lights to enhance production quality.

2. Experiment With Angles:
   - Add variety with dynamic camera angles, zoom-ins, or transitions.

3. Leverage TikTok Filters and Effects:
   - Use trending effects to enhance your videos creatively.

6. Keep It Short and Sweet

TikTok videos are short by design. Less is often more:

1. Avoid Filler Content:
   - Get straight to the point.

2. Focus on a Single Idea:
   - Example: Instead of listing "10 Ways to Save Money," focus on one tip per video.

3. Use Quick Edits:
   - Maintain energy with snappy cuts and transitions.

7. Add Calls-to-Action (CTAs)

Drive engagement by prompting viewers to take action:

1. Direct CTAs:
   - Examples: "Follow for more tips," "Share if this helped," or "Comment your favorite part."

2. Subtle CTAs:
   - Embed prompts within your narrative. For instance, ask a question in your video to encourage comments.

8. Optimize for the Algorithm
Understanding TikTok's algorithm ensures your content gets the visibility it deserves:
1. Leverage Keywords:
   - Use relevant keywords in captions and hashtags to make your videos discoverable.

2. Post Consistently:
   - Regular posting keeps your account active in the algorithm's eyes.

3. Engage With Your Audience:
   - Responding to comments and interacting with viewers increases engagement rates.

9. Learn From Analytics
TikTok's analytics tools offer invaluable insights:
1. Track Performance:
   - Identify your most successful videos and analyze why they performed well.

2. Audience Insights:
   - Adjust content based on viewer demographics and preferences.

10. Experiment and Adapt
Success on TikTok requires flexibility and creativity:
1. Test New Ideas:
   - Regularly try different formats, styles, or themes.

2. Learn From Others:
   - Observe popular creators and incorporate techniques that align with your style.

3. Evolve With Trends:
   - Continuously adapt to TikTok's shifting culture and trends.

Case Study: A Creator's Rise to Viral Fame
Creator: A fashion stylist who combines humor and style tips.
Strategy:
1. Uses a consistent hook: "Here's how to NOT dress like a disaster."
2. Leverages storytelling by critiquing outfits humorously.
3. Engages viewers with a CTA: "Which outfit is worse? Comment below!"
   Result: Millions of followers and a loyal community.

The Boomer Bottom Line
Creating engaging TikTok content is an art that combines strategy with creativity. By mastering hooks, trends, storytelling, and visual appeal, you can captivate your audience and carve a niche on this dynamic platform. In the next chapter, we'll ex-

plore how to navigate TikTok's monetization opportunities and turn your creative efforts into tangible rewards.

Chapter 8: How to Monetize Your TikTok Content

TikTok offers more than just creative expression - it's also a platform for monetizing your influence. Whether you're a hobbyist looking for a side income or an aspiring influencer aiming to turn your TikTok presence into a full-time job, understanding how to effectively monetize your content is essential. In this chapter, we'll dive into various monetization strategies, from brand partnerships and affiliate marketing to TikTok's native creator tools, helping you transform your passion into profit.

1. TikTok Creator Fund: How It Works

The TikTok Creator Fund is one of the primary ways users can earn money directly from the platform. This fund is based on video performance, and while the payouts may vary, understanding how it works is key.

How to Join the TikTok Creator Fund:
1. Eligibility: To join, you need to:
   - Be at least 18 years old.
   - Have at least 10,000 followers.
   - Have at least 100,000 video views in the last 30 days.
   - Adhere to TikTok's Community Guidelines.

2. How It Pays:
   - Payments are based on factors like video views, engagement rates, and content originality. The more popular your videos, the higher your payout.
   - Keep in mind that the per-view payout is relatively small, so consistency and engagement are key.

3. Maximizing Earnings with the Fund:
   - Focus on high-engagement content: Videos with strong engagement (likes, comments, shares) perform better.
   - Post regularly: Consistent posting increases your chances of being seen and rewarded by the algorithm.

2. Brand Partnerships and Sponsored Content

Brand partnerships are another lucrative way to monetize your TikTok presence. Brands are increasingly turning to influencers for authentic promotion, and TikTok is no exception.

How to Land Brand Partnerships:
1. Build Your Brand: Brands typically look for influencers with a distinct niche and engaged audience. Define your niche (fashion, fitness, tech, etc.), and tailor your content to appeal to both your audience and potential sponsors.
2. Reach Out to Brands: Once you've built a significant following, you can approach brands for collaborations. Include statistics like engagement rates and follower demographics to show your value.
3. Use Influencer Platforms: Platforms like Influence.co, AspireIQ, and Grapevine Village can connect you with brands looking for TikTok influencers.

4. Negotiating Sponsored Posts: When negotiating with brands, ensure you are clear about your deliverables, such as how many videos you will produce, the number of posts, and any content guidelines.

What to Keep in Mind:
- Authenticity: Your audience values authenticity, so it's important to only promote products or services you truly believe in.
- Disclosure: Always disclose paid partnerships using TikTok's built-in "Branded Content" tool to avoid any confusion or backlash.

3. Affiliate Marketing

Affiliate marketing allows you to earn commissions by promoting products through special affiliate links. If someone buys the product using your link, you earn a percentage of the sale.

How to Start with Affiliate Marketing:
1. Join Affiliate Programs: Popular affiliate programs like Amazon Associates, ShareASale, and Rakuten allow creators to generate affiliate links for products.
2. Incorporate Affiliate Links in Your Content: Create content that naturally incorporates the products you are promoting. For example, a beauty influencer might create tutorials featuring products with affiliate links.
3. Use TikTok's Link Feature: TikTok allows users to add a link in their bio, which is perfect for sharing affiliate links.

Tips for Success:
- Disclose Affiliations: Be transparent with your audience about affiliate links.
- Be Selective: Choose products that fit your niche and would appeal to your audience to maintain trust.

4. Selling Your Own Products or Services

If you have your own brand, products, or services, TikTok can be an excellent platform to promote and sell them.

How to Sell on TikTok:
1. Set Up Your Store: You can sell products directly through TikTok's integration with Shopify or TikTok Shop, which allows creators to add a product carousel to their profile or videos.
2. Create Engaging Content: Use videos to showcase your products in action. Product demos, behind-the-scenes, and how-to videos are excellent ways to build interest.
3. Leverage TikTok Ads: TikTok offers ad tools for creators to promote their products more widely. In-Feed Ads, Branded Hashtag Challenges, and Top View Ads are some of the options to consider.

Examples:
- A fitness influencer could sell workout plans or custom workout gear.
- A fashion creator might promote a clothing line or accessories.

5. Live Gifts and Donations

TikTok's live streaming feature allows creators to receive gifts from viewers during live broadcasts. These gifts are purchased with TikTok coins and can be redeemed for real money.

How to Use Live Gifts for Monetization:
1. Host Engaging Lives: Go live regularly and engage with your audience. Hold Q&A sessions, create challenges, or offer live tutorials.
2. Promote the Gift Feature: Remind your viewers that they can send gifts during the stream, but always ensure it feels natural.

6. Offering Paid Subscriptions

TikTok introduced the TikTok Subscriptions feature, where creators can charge their followers for exclusive content, offering a more direct way to monetize.

How to Use TikTok Subscriptions:
1. Offer Exclusive Content: Subscribers get access to behind-the-scenes content, tutorials, or other special videos not available to the general public.
2. Engage Your Subscribers: Offer value by regularly updating exclusive content and interacting with your paying audience.

7. Crowdfunding and Patreon

If you're producing content consistently, crowdfunding (arranged via third-party sites but promoted along with your TikTok activity) can be another option for monetization.

1. Patreon: Patreon allows creators to set up membership tiers where followers can pay for exclusive content.
2. Kickstarter or GoFundMe: For special projects or content creation goals, you can use crowdfunding platforms to fund your TikTok content creation.

8. Creating a Paid TikTok Course or Coaching Program

Once you've established yourself as an expert in a particular area, consider creating a paid course or coaching program. Whether it's teaching makeup tips, fitness routines, or even how to grow on TikTok, the possibilities are vast.

How to Create and Sell a Course:
1. Create a Value Proposition: Offer something unique that will attract paying customers.
2. Platform Options: Use platforms like Teachable, Udemy, or Kajabi to host and sell your course.
3. Promote It on TikTok: Use your TikTok content to showcase snippets of your course or provide insights to draw in potential customers.

9. Collaborating with Other Creators

Collaborations open the door for joint monetization efforts and can exponentially grow your reach. Collaborating with fellow creators can bring in new followers, sponsors, and opportunities.

How to Collaborate for Profit:
1. Find Like-Minded Creators: Look for creators with similar interests or audiences.

2. Create Joint Content: Consider running live sessions, challenges, or duets.
3. Leverage Each Other's Audiences: Cross-promote content to reach new followers and increase your potential earnings.

The Boomer Bottom Line

Monetizing your TikTok presence is entirely possible, but it requires a strategy that aligns with your content, audience, and goals. By diversifying your income streams - whether through the Creator Fund, brand partnerships, selling products, or live gifts - you can start earning while continuing to focus on creating content you love. Stay authentic, engage with your audience, and use the tools TikTok provides to ensure you're maximizing your potential for income.

Chapter 9: Advanced TikTok Strategies for Going Viral

Every TikTok creator dreams of going viral - but achieving viral status isn't as simple as posting any random video. It requires a deep understanding of the platform's algorithms, content trends, audience behavior, and more. In this chapter, we'll explore advanced strategies to increase your chances of going viral on TikTok, helping you take your content to the next level.

1. Understanding the TikTok Algorithm

To create viral content, you first need to understand how TikTok's algorithm works. The platform uses a highly personalized recommendation system, which means that your videos are shown to users based on a variety of factors.

Key Factors Affecting the TikTok Algorithm:
1. User Interactions: Likes, comments, shares, and video rewatches signal to the algorithm that a video is worth promoting.
2. Video Information: This includes captions, hashtags, sounds, and effects. The algorithm uses this data to match your content with relevant audiences.
3. Device and Account Settings: These factors, like your device type, language preferences, and location, influence who sees your content.

How to Optimize for the Algorithm:
- Use Trending Sounds: Keep an eye on viral sounds and integrate them into your videos. TikTok's algorithm tends to favor content that uses popular sounds.
- Craft Engaging Captions: Keep your captions intriguing and ask questions to encourage interaction.
- Hashtags: Use relevant and trending hashtags to make sure your content reaches a larger audience. Don't overuse hashtags; instead, focus on a balance of niche and popular ones.

2. Leverage TikTok's "For You" Page

The coveted For You Page (FYP) is where viral content typically gets its start. Here, TikTok curates a personalized feed for each user, showcasing videos they might enjoy based on their interactions and preferences.

How to Get Featured on the FYP:
1. Create Highly Shareable Content: Videos that provoke a strong emotional response—whether that's humor, awe, or surprise—tend to be shared more.
2. Optimize Video Length: TikTok users generally engage more with shorter videos, especially ones that are under 15 seconds.
3. Timing Matters: Posting at peak times when your target audience is most active increases your chances of being featured.

Tip: Analyze the performance of your posts and try to determine what type of content resonates most with your followers.

3. Utilizing TikTok Challenges and Trends

Participating in challenges is one of the fastest ways to get noticed on TikTok, and if you can add a unique spin to a viral trend, your video may gain extra attention.

How to Ride the Trend Wave:
1. Follow Trend Hashtags: Keep an eye on trending hashtags or challenges. TikTok usually highlights trending challenges on the "Discover" page.
2. Add a Creative Twist: Don't just repeat the challenge—add your own unique flair or perspective. It's the creative and unexpected spins that often gain the most attention.
3. Timing: As with trending sounds, timing is key. Join a trend as soon as it picks up steam to increase your chances of viral success.

4. Mastering TikTok Video Editing and Effects

TikTok offers a variety of creative tools to enhance your videos. Learning how to use these tools to elevate your content can make a significant difference in your chances of going viral.

Essential Editing Techniques:
1. Transitions: Smooth and creative transitions make your video visually appealing and encourage viewers to keep watching. Experiment with the wide array of transitions TikTok offers.
2. Effects and Filters: Use these to enhance your video's aesthetic or to add a fun element. Effects like slow-motion, green screen, or face filters can make your video stand out.
3. Text and Captions: Adding text overlays can make your video more engaging, especially when they align with the video's narrative. Keep it concise and on-brand.

5. Collaborating with Other Creators

Collaborating with other TikTok creators is a powerful way to amplify your reach. It's not just about sharing followers—it's about exchanging creativity and expanding your content's visibility.

How to Collaborate Effectively:
1. Choose Partners Wisely: Collaborate with creators who share a similar niche or audience. This increases the likelihood that their followers will be interested in your content.
2. Create Engaging Duets or Stitches: TikTok allows you to respond to or react to other users' videos using the Duet or Stitch features. This can drive engagement and expand your exposure to new followers.
3. Host Challenges Together: Create a collaborative challenge with another creator. This allows you both to tap into each other's audiences and gain more visibility.

6. Audience Engagement and Community Building

Creating viral content is about more than just posting—it's about building a community of engaged followers who want to interact with you.

How to Build an Engaged Community:

1. Respond to Comments: Take the time to respond to your followers' comments. This shows that you care about your audience and helps foster a loyal following.
2. Host Giveaways: Run giveaways and contests to incentivize engagement. People love free stuff, and this can encourage more comments, shares, and follows.
3. Engage in Conversations: Don't just post content—actively participate in discussions with your followers. This humanizes your profile and makes it easier for people to relate to you.

7. Experiment with Different Content Types

To find what works best for your audience and TikTok's algorithm, experiment with various types of content. From tutorials to comedy skits, there are numerous options for experimentation.

Types of Content to Experiment With:
1. Educational Content: Tutorials or "how-to" videos can go viral, especially if they offer valuable information in an entertaining format.
2. Storytelling: Sharing personal stories or unique experiences often resonates with audiences. Narratives draw people in and encourage them to watch until the end.
3. Humor and Memes: Comedy is one of TikTok's most popular categories. Funny skits, memes, or reactions often generate significant engagement.

8. Cross-Promote on Other Platforms

TikTok content doesn't have to live exclusively on TikTok. Cross-promotion can help you reach new audiences who may not have discovered you yet.

How to Cross-Promote Your TikTok:
1. Share TikToks on Instagram: Instagram Stories or Reels are perfect places to repost your TikTok videos.
2. Use Twitter and Facebook: Share clips or snippets of your TikTok content to encourage your followers on other platforms to check out your full TikTok account.
3. Collaborate with YouTube: If you're already creating longer-form content for YouTube, embed your TikTok videos or link to your TikTok profile in your video descriptions.

The Boomer Bottom Line

Going viral on TikTok is not a matter of luck—it's a science, a combination of the right timing, creativity, and audience engagement. By understanding the algorithm, mastering content trends, and actively engaging with your community, you can drastically increase your chances of viral success. Remember that the more authentic and unique your content is, the more likely it is to resonate with TikTok's diverse and enthusiastic user base.

Chapter 10: TikTok for Personal and Professional Growth

TikTok is more than just a platform for entertainment—it's a powerful tool for personal development and business growth. With its ability to connect creators to global audiences, TikTok has become a prime space for individuals to develop their skills, increase their confidence, and expand their professional networks. In this chapter, we'll explore how TikTok can be leveraged for both personal and professional growth, from marketing a business to boosting creativity and confidence. We'll also look at some success stories of creators who started small and grew their presence through the app.

1. Leveraging TikTok for Business Marketing
As TikTok has evolved, businesses of all sizes have recognized its potential for marketing. It provides an opportunity to connect with a younger demographic, increase brand awareness, and generate engagement in ways that traditional advertising can't match. But businesses don't need to have massive budgets or large followings to succeed on TikTok - creativity is the key.

How Businesses Use TikTok:
1. Creating Engaging, Short-Form Content: Unlike long-form platforms like YouTube, TikTok is focused on quick, consumable content. Businesses need to think creatively about how to make their products or services appear entertaining while still communicating their value.
   - For example, businesses in the fashion industry might use TikTok to show off their clothing through fun, trendy videos, while beauty brands can demonstrate makeup tutorials or skincare routines.

2. Leveraging Trends and Challenges: TikTok thrives on viral trends and challenges, and businesses can use these to their advantage. Participating in viral challenges can help a brand gain visibility and connect with potential customers in a lighthearted way. Brands like Gymshark, for example, have successfully used influencer partnerships to tap into challenges relevant to fitness and wellness.

3. Influencer Partnerships: Influencers are often seen as more relatable and trustworthy than traditional ads, which is why they are an essential part of any TikTok marketing strategy. Brands partner with creators whose personal brand aligns with their own to reach new audiences.
   - Chipotle and The Washington Post are great examples of businesses that have successfully used TikTok influencers to reach younger, more engaged audiences.

4. Paid Advertising on TikTok: TikTok offers several forms of paid advertising, including In-Feed Ads, Branded Hashtag Challenges, and TopView Ads. These can help businesses reach specific demographics, encourage user engagement, and increase brand visibility.

- In-Feed Ads appear in users' main feeds and are the most common type of advertisement. They blend seamlessly into the content, making them less intrusive than traditional ads.
- Hashtag Challenges encourage user-generated content and increase the chances of your campaign going viral, especially if you offer rewards or incentives for participating.

2. Personal Development: Creativity, Confidence, and Networking

Beyond business marketing, TikTok is a treasure trove for personal development. The app offers opportunities for individuals to nurture creativity, boost confidence, and build meaningful professional networks. Whether you want to express your creativity, gain confidence in front of the camera, or connect with like-minded professionals, TikTok can help you grow.

Creativity:
TikTok encourages creativity in a way that few other platforms do. With its vast array of filters, sounds, and editing tools, users can explore their creative side by making videos that entertain, inform, or inspire.
- Creative Expression: Whether you're an aspiring comedian, artist, or musician, TikTok allows you to create and share content that represents your passion. The app's interactive features, such as duets and stitches, enable creators to collaborate with others and experiment with new ideas.
- Storytelling: TikTok's short-form video format forces creators to focus on storytelling. This develops a more concise and impactful communication style, an invaluable skill both personally and professionally.

Confidence:
One of the unexpected benefits of creating content on TikTok is that it can help you build confidence. By putting yourself out there and sharing your ideas, you will inevitably face feedback, both positive and negative. Over time, this helps you become more resilient and self-assured in your abilities.
- Comfort with the Camera: Many people feel self-conscious when they first start recording videos. TikTok provides an easy way to practice and improve your on-camera presence, whether it's through informational videos or lighthearted content. The more you create, the more comfortable you'll become with the process.
- Feedback and Growth: Constructive criticism from viewers can help you grow and improve your content. Embracing feedback (both positive and negative) builds self-confidence and encourages self-improvement.

Networking:
TikTok isn't just about creating content—it's also a space for building relationships and professional networking. The app's algorithm connects people from diverse backgrounds, and creators often form meaningful connections in their niches.
- Building a Community: As you grow your following on TikTok, you naturally build a community of like-minded individuals. Engage with your followers by responding to comments, joining live streams, and collaborating on videos. This connec-

tion fosters a sense of belonging and allows you to build relationships that can lead to new opportunities.
- Connecting with Industry Professionals: TikTok can serve as an informal networking tool. Many professionals, including musicians, educators, and marketers, are on the platform, using it to share tips, trends, and advice. By engaging with others in your industry, you can learn from their experiences and even discover opportunities for collaboration.

3. Examples of Successful TikTokers Who Started Small

Many of TikTok's most successful creators began with small followings and have since turned their accounts into full-fledged businesses or careers. Their stories highlight how TikTok can be a powerful platform for growth, regardless of where you start.

1. Charli D'Amelio:
Charli D'Amelio is perhaps the most famous example of TikTok success. She started by posting dance videos and, within a year, became the most followed user on the platform. Charli has since expanded her brand by collaborating with companies like Dunkin' Donuts and investing in a reality show. Her story exemplifies how anyone can start small, develop their skills, and reach massive audiences.

2. Addison Rae:
Addison Rae initially gained popularity on TikTok for her dance choreography videos. As her following grew, she expanded into acting, launched a podcast, and even signed a major deal with Netflix. Addison's success on TikTok has propelled her into mainstream media, showing that the platform can be a launching pad for broader opportunities.

3. Khaby Lame:
Khaby Lame went viral for his unique approach to solving overly complicated life hacks with simple, straightforward solutions. He became a sensation by staying true to his personality and approach, demonstrating that creativity and authenticity can lead to viral success—even without flashy production values or high-budget content.

4. Dr. Julie Smith:
Dr. Julie Smith, a clinical psychologist, leveraged TikTok to share mental health tips and advice. Her calm, insightful approach to mental health topics resonated with millions. She now has a large following and uses her platform to advocate for mental well-being and provide valuable resources to her audience.

The Boomer Bottom Line

TikTok is not just a fun app for dancing and lip-syncing—it's a tool for growth, both personal and professional. From building a business presence to enhancing your creativity and confidence, the platform offers an abundance of opportunities for anyone willing to put in the effort. By embracing TikTok's unique features, creators can achieve both personal fulfillment and business success.

As TikTok continues to evolve, its potential for self-expression, professional networking, and brand-building will only grow. By understanding how to navigate the app effectively, you can use it as a launchpad for your own growth and success, regardless of whether you're building a personal brand, launching a business, or simply looking to expand your horizons.

Chapter 11: Advanced Features and Analytics

Mastering TikTok goes beyond simply posting videos - it's about understanding the platform's advanced features and leveraging TikTok's built-in tools and analytics to refine your strategy and increase engagement. Whether you're a business or an individual creator, diving deeper into the platform's capabilities can help you grow your presence, optimize your content, and track your performance effectively. In this chapter, we will cover advanced tools like Stitch, Duet, and Live, and explore how to use TikTok Analytics to fine-tune your strategy. Additionally, we'll discuss integrating TikTok with other platforms like Instagram and YouTube to expand your reach.

1. Using TikTok Analytics to Improve Performance

TikTok's built-in analytics tool offers creators valuable insights that can help them track performance, understand audience demographics, and improve content strategy. The key to success on TikTok, especially for creators and businesses aiming to grow, is understanding the data that the platform provides and using it to adapt and improve.

Accessing TikTok Analytics:
To access TikTok Analytics, you need to switch to a Pro Account, which is free and available to anyone. Here's how you can set up your Pro account:
1. Go to your profile and tap on the three dots in the top right corner.
2. Under "Manage Account," select "Switch to Pro Account."
3. Choose whether you want a Creator or Business Account, depending on your goals.

Once you've set up your Pro Account, you can access your analytics by going to your profile and tapping on the "Analytics" option.

Key Metrics in TikTok Analytics:
TikTok Analytics offers three main sections: Overview, Content, and Followers.
1. Overview:
   - Video Views: Tracks how many times your videos have been viewed in the past 7 or 28 days. This is a key metric to assess how much reach your content is getting.
   - Profile Views: This measures how many people have visited your profile, indicating how much your content is driving traffic to your account.
   - Followers: Insights into your follower growth over time. This can help you see trends and determine what type of content attracts new followers.

2. Content:
   - Video Performance: You can see the performance of your individual videos, including likes, comments, shares, and total views. This is crucial for understanding what works best for your audience.
   - Trending Content: TikTok highlights the content that is currently performing well. This can give you a sense of what's trending and allow you to capitalize on viral topics.

3. Followers:

- Demographics: Get insights into the gender, age range, and location of your followers. Understanding who your audience is can help you tailor your content more effectively.
- Activity: See when your followers are most active on the platform. This information is useful for scheduling your posts to maximize engagement.

Using Analytics for Strategy:
- Identify High-Performing Content: By looking at what types of videos receive the most engagement, you can replicate those styles or themes in future content. If dance videos get more views, try adding them to your content strategy.
- Optimize Post Timing: By examining when your followers are most active, you can plan your uploads for those peak times, increasing the likelihood of engagement.
- Track Growth: Regularly review your follower growth and compare it to the content you've posted. If you notice a jump in followers after posting certain types of content, try producing more of that type to build momentum.

2. Tools like Stitch, Duet, and Live for Audience Engagement

TikTok offers several powerful features that encourage interaction and community building. The platform's tools like Stitch, Duet, and Live provide great ways to engage with other creators, collaborate, and deepen connections with your audience.

Stitch:
The Stitch feature allows you to take a part of another user's video and incorporate it into your own. This is an excellent way to engage with other creators, remix content, and add your own unique twist to popular trends.
- How to Use Stitch: Tap on the "Share" button of a video and select "Stitch." You can then trim a section of the video (up to 5 seconds) and add your own reaction or extension to it. This makes for engaging and interactive content.
- Best Practices:
  - Be respectful when stitching other creators' content. Always ensure that you're adding value with your own perspective or interpretation.
  - Use this feature for reactions, critiques, or adding your thoughts to existing trends, which can foster more community interactions.

Duet:
Duet lets you create a split-screen video with another user's content. It's similar to Stitch, but instead of directly integrating the original video into yours, it shows both videos side-by-side. This can be a great way to collaborate, create challenges, or participate in trends.
- How to Use Duet: Find a video you'd like to interact with, tap the "Share" button, and select "Duet." You can then record your part alongside the original video. This feature is perfect for showcasing your reaction, singing alongside someone, or even performing a challenge with another user.
- Best Practices:
  - Collaborative Challenges: Use Duet to participate in or create challenges, where others can join in on the fun. This encourages community participation and increases visibility.

- **Engage Creatively:** Don't just duplicate the original content; bring your unique flair to the duet. For instance, you can add humor, improve on a dance move, or add a counterpoint to a point made in the original video.

Live:
Going Live on TikTok allows creators to interact with their audience in real-time. It's a great way to build a deeper connection with followers and show your authentic self.
- **How to Use Live:** To start a live stream, tap the "+" button, select "Go Live," and follow the prompts. You can interact with your viewers through comments, answer questions, and even receive virtual gifts from your followers.
- **Best Practices:**
  - **Regular Live Sessions:** Consistency is key for successful live streaming. Create a regular schedule for your live sessions to build anticipation.
  - **Engage with Your Audience:** The best live sessions are interactive. Respond to comments, ask questions, and make your followers feel involved.
  - **Monetization:** If you have enough followers, you can start receiving virtual gifts from viewers, which can be converted into real money. This makes Live a potential revenue stream for creators.

3. Integrating TikTok with Other Platforms (Instagram, YouTube)

While TikTok itself is an incredibly powerful platform, integrating it with other social media channels can significantly amplify your reach and help grow your presence across multiple platforms. Instagram and YouTube are two platforms that work particularly well alongside TikTok.

TikTok and Instagram:
- **Cross-Promotion:** Use Instagram to showcase snippets of your TikTok videos or share TikTok content directly in your Instagram Stories. This encourages your followers on Instagram to check out your TikTok profile and potentially follow you there.
- **Instagram Reels:** Instagram's Reels feature is very similar to TikTok. By repurposing your TikTok content for Instagram Reels, you can reach a broader audience without creating entirely new videos.
- **Linking to TikTok:** Always include your TikTok handle in your Instagram bio and vice versa to make it easy for followers on one platform to find you on the other.

TikTok and YouTube:
- **YouTube Shorts:** Much like Instagram Reels, YouTube Shorts can be used to repurpose your TikTok videos. This expands your content to a new audience, leveraging YouTube's massive platform.
- **Cross-Promote:** Use YouTube for longer-form content and direct traffic to your TikTok. For example, if you're creating a vlog or tutorial, you can link to your TikTok at the end, encouraging viewers to follow you there for bite-sized content.
- **Promote YouTube Videos on TikTok:** If you've uploaded a new YouTube video, create a teaser or snippet for TikTok to drive traffic to your YouTube channel. This

can be especially useful for tutorial-based or in-depth content that works better on YouTube.

The Boomer Bottom Line

Mastering TikTok goes beyond basic content creation; it's about leveraging its advanced features, understanding analytics, and integrating it seamlessly into your broader social media strategy. By utilizing TikTok's powerful tools like Stitch, Duet, and Live, you can foster engagement, collaborate with other creators, and build a community around your content. Additionally, using TikTok Analytics helps you refine your approach, track your performance, and continually improve.

Moreover, TikTok's integration with other platforms like Instagram and YouTube expands your reach and allows for cross-platform promotion, creating a unified digital presence. Whether you're a business looking to market products or an individual aiming to grow your personal brand, understanding these advanced features and strategies is essential to your TikTok success.

Chapter 12: Common Challenges and Solutions

While TikTok offers incredible opportunities for content creation and audience engagement, it also presents its fair share of challenges. As you work to build a presence, you may encounter negative comments, struggles with balancing your time, or technical issues that threaten your creative flow. This chapter will explore common problems faced by creators on TikTok and provide solutions to help you overcome them. Whether you're dealing with online negativity, screen burnout, or technical hiccups, knowing how to address these challenges can make your TikTok experience more enjoyable and productive.

1. Dealing with Negative Comments and Trolls

As with any social media platform, TikTok can expose creators to negative comments, trolls, and online harassment. While the vast majority of comments are positive, the occasional unkind or cruel remark can still take a toll on your confidence and motivation. Here's how to effectively deal with negativity:
Understanding the Source of Negative Comments:
- Trolls and Hatred: Trolls often thrive on provoking reactions. These individuals aren't typically genuine in their criticism but are instead attempting to draw attention through negative remarks.
- Jealousy or Envy: Creators with rapidly growing followings or viral videos may attract envy or jealousy, leading some users to leave discouraging or harmful comments.
- Misunderstandings or Misinterpretations: Sometimes, the tone or intent of a comment can be misconstrued. What may seem negative might just be a poor choice of words or a difference in communication style.

Strategies for Handling Negative Comments:
- Don't Engage with Trolls: One of the best ways to handle trolls is to simply ignore them. Responding to trolls typically fuels their behavior, giving them the attention they crave. Instead, focus on the positive feedback from your audience.
- Block and Report: If comments cross the line into harassment or hate speech, it's essential to block and report the user to TikTok. The platform has tools for reporting bullying, hate speech, and other inappropriate content, helping to keep the community safe.
- Mute or Filter Comments: TikTok allows you to mute or filter certain keywords from your comments section. You can also disable comments altogether for specific videos if you feel the need to avoid negativity. These tools help create a more controlled and positive environment.
- Focus on the Positive: Instead of dwelling on the negativity, focus on the positive interactions with your supporters. Acknowledge and thank your followers who offer constructive feedback and encouragement.

Real-World Example:
Many TikTokers, including famous creators like Charli D'Amelio and Addison Rae, have openly discussed the emotional toll of dealing with online hate. In response, they've implemented strategies like setting boundaries with their audiences, focus-

ing on self-care, and seeking support from friends, family, and mental health professionals.

2. Balancing Screen Time and Avoiding Burnout

TikTok can be incredibly time-consuming, especially when you're dedicated to creating multiple pieces of content each day. While the app is designed for quick consumption, it can quickly become addictive. Balancing screen time and avoiding burnout are essential for maintaining both your physical and mental well-being.

Signs of Burnout:
- Loss of Creativity: Feeling uninspired or unable to come up with fresh content ideas is a common symptom of burnout. This can happen when you push yourself too hard or too fast to keep up with the demands of constant posting.
- Fatigue: If you're feeling mentally or physically exhausted after spending long hours creating and consuming content, it's a clear sign that you need to take a break.
- Stress and Anxiety: The pressure to maintain a consistent posting schedule, engage with followers, and meet expectations can create significant stress. If left unchecked, this can lead to anxiety or feelings of inadequacy.

Strategies for Managing Screen Time and Avoiding Burnout:
- Set Boundaries: Establish clear boundaries around your TikTok usage. For instance, allocate specific hours during the day for content creation and engagement, then disconnect. Allow yourself to recharge without the constant pull of social media.
- Batch Your Content: Rather than creating and posting content every day, batch your filming and editing sessions. Dedicate specific days to shooting multiple videos, and schedule them to be posted at optimal times. This allows you to rest on off days and prevents burnout from constant daily posting.
- Take Breaks: Incorporating regular breaks is crucial for avoiding burnout. Take time to rest, engage in hobbies, or spend time with loved ones without the distraction of TikTok. Sometimes, stepping away from the screen for a day or two can help reignite your creativity.
- Engage in Other Forms of Content Creation: Diversifying your creative output can help refresh your approach. Try creating content for other platforms, like YouTube, Instagram, or even writing blogs. This can bring a sense of novelty and break the monotony of TikTok creation.

Real-World Example:
Creators like Hannah Stocking and Zach King have shared how they manage their mental health by taking breaks from TikTok or focusing on other platforms when they feel burnout creeping in. Zach King, for example, is known for his high-quality editing and magic-based content, but he has spoken about how he occasionally steps away from the app to prevent burnout.

3. Troubleshooting Technical Issues

TikTok is a fast-paced platform that relies heavily on video creation and editing, so technical issues can sometimes cause frustration for creators. Whether it's problems with video uploading, audio sync issues, or the app not responding, it's important to know how to troubleshoot these problems efficiently.

Common Technical Issues on TikTok:
1. Videos Won't Upload: Sometimes, videos refuse to upload or remain stuck on "Processing." This could be due to app glitches, slow internet connections, or issues with the video format.
2. Audio Issues: Audio may not sync correctly with the video, or it may be out of sync altogether, leading to a jarring viewing experience.
3. App Freezing or Crashing: Occasionally, TikTok may freeze or crash during use, especially when too many apps or browser tabs are open at once.
4. Low-Quality Video: Videos may lose resolution when uploaded to TikTok, affecting the visual quality of your content.

Solutions for Technical Problems:
- Clear Cache: Go to the app settings, clear the app cache, and restart TikTok. This can resolve many issues related to lagging, freezing, and slow uploads.
- Check Your Internet Connection: Ensure you have a stable internet connection. If you're using mobile data, switch to Wi-Fi, or vice versa, to see if the connection improves.
- Update TikTok: If the app is crashing or not functioning properly, check for updates. Keeping TikTok updated ensures that you're using the most recent version, which is optimized for performance.
- Video Resolution: If your videos are uploading in poor quality, ensure that they are shot in high resolution (1080p or above) and that you're not compressing the video too much before uploading.
- Restart Your Device: Sometimes, simply restarting your phone or tablet can resolve issues with apps freezing or not functioning correctly.

Real-World Example:
Several creators have encountered issues with the app freezing when trying to upload videos. In a widely circulated Reddit thread, users shared how clearing the cache and reinstalling the app helped them resolve upload issues. Additionally, YouTube tutorials often emphasize the importance of updating both the app and your phone's operating system to prevent performance glitches.

The Boomer Bottom Line

While TikTok is a fun and exciting platform, creators must be prepared to deal with the challenges it brings. Negative comments, burnout, and technical issues are part of the TikTok journey, but with the right strategies, you can navigate these obstacles with confidence. By focusing on positivity and creativity, setting clear boundaries, and knowing how to troubleshoot problems efficiently, you can continue to grow your presence and enjoy your experience on the platform.

Chapter 13: TikTok Etiquette and Safety

As TikTok continues to grow in popularity, it's becoming more important than ever to maintain respectful interactions and ensure the safety of both creators and viewers. The platform is home to a diverse community of people from all walks of life, so understanding TikTok etiquette and the policies surrounding it is essential for fostering a positive, enjoyable experience for everyone. Additionally, ensuring your privacy and security while engaging on the app is crucial, particularly given the amount of personal data shared on social media. This chapter will guide you through TikTok's community guidelines, best practices for respectful interactions, and strategies to protect your privacy and security on the platform.

1. TikTok Community Guidelines and Policies

Understanding TikTok's community guidelines is key to having a positive presence on the platform. These guidelines set the tone for appropriate content and behavior and help ensure that all users can engage in a safe, respectful environment. Violating these guidelines can lead to content removal or even account suspension, so it's important to stay informed.

TikTok's Core Principles:
TikTok's community guidelines are designed to promote creativity and authenticity while ensuring that users interact safely and respectfully. Some core principles include:

- Safety: Content that promotes harmful behavior, bullying, or violence is strictly prohibited. TikTok has a zero-tolerance policy for hate speech, threats, and content that encourages self-harm.
- Respect: TikTok encourages respect for others' opinions, identities, and cultures. Discrimination, harassment, or targeted abuse is not permitted on the platform.
- Transparency: TikTok works to create a transparent environment by moderating content and enforcing policies consistently to maintain fairness.
- Fun and Creative Expression: TikTok's primary goal is to allow users to share their creativity. It encourages freedom of expression within the boundaries of safety and respect.

Key Guidelines to Follow:
- Hate Speech and Harassment: TikTok has strict policies against hate speech, racism, sexism, and any form of discriminatory behavior. Negative, harmful, or abusive language targeting individuals or groups based on race, religion, gender, or sexual orientation is prohibited.
- Violence and Dangerous Behavior: Content promoting violence, the glorification of self-harm, or harmful challenges is banned. Users must refrain from posting content that could incite violence or encourage dangerous behavior.
- Nudity and Sexual Content: TikTok does not allow sexually explicit content, nudity, or any type of suggestive material meant to provoke or exploit users. The platform adheres to a strict policy that keeps interactions appropriate for users of all ages.
- Misinformation: TikTok actively works to reduce the spread of misinformation, especially related to public health and political matters. Content that spreads false

or misleading information may be removed or flagged by TikTok's moderation system.

Real-World Example: One example of TikTok enforcing its guidelines occurred during the COVID-19 pandemic when the platform actively flagged and removed content that promoted misinformation about the virus or its vaccines. This effort is part of TikTok's broader commitment to preventing the spread of false information and keeping the community safe.

2. Best Practices for Respectful Interactions

Engaging with others respectfully is essential for building a positive and welcoming TikTok community. Here are several best practices for maintaining respectful interactions on the platform:

Respectful Comments:
- Be Positive and Constructive: When engaging in the comment sections, aim to be encouraging, thoughtful, and constructive. If you disagree with someone's point of view, express your opinion respectfully without resorting to personal attacks.
- Report Inappropriate Content: If you encounter content that violates TikTok's guidelines, such as hate speech, harassment, or explicit material, use the report feature to alert TikTok's moderators. This helps keep the platform safe for everyone.
- Avoid Cyberbullying: Cyberbullying can be a serious issue on social media, and TikTok is no exception. If you see someone being targeted with harassment or abuse, either avoid engaging or, when appropriate, offer positive reinforcement to counter the negativity.
- Use Humor Wisely: Humor can be a great tool for engaging with others, but it can also easily be misinterpreted. Avoid humor that might be offensive or hurtful to others, especially in a diverse community like TikTok's.

Building Community and Respecting Boundaries:
- Engage with Others Genuinely: Build authentic relationships with your followers and fellow creators by interacting genuinely. Whether through comments, Duets, or collaborations, aim to uplift and support the people you interact with.
- Respect User Privacy: If you're creating content that involves others, always respect their boundaries. Don't share private information, images, or videos of others without permission. When collaborating, make sure all parties are comfortable with how they'll be portrayed in your content.

Real-World Example:
Creators like Josh Richards and Charli D'Amelio often emphasize kindness and positivity in their content and interactions. Charli has discussed how she engages with her followers by maintaining a friendly and approachable demeanor, while Josh Richards promotes positive messaging and mental health awareness within the TikTok community.

3. Ensuring Privacy and Security on TikTok

While TikTok is a fun and creative platform, it's important to be mindful of privacy and security. Given the amount of personal data shared on social media, protecting your information is crucial for safeguarding your online presence.

Protecting Your Personal Information:
- Limit What You Share: Be cautious about the personal information you post, such as your full name, address, phone number, or financial details. TikTok allows you to control how much personal information is visible to others.
- Adjust Your Privacy Settings: TikTok offers various privacy settings that you can adjust to protect your account. You can make your account private, limit who can comment on your videos, or restrict who can send you direct messages.
  - Private Account: If your account is set to private, only people who you approve as followers can see your videos and interact with you.
  - Restricted Content: You can control who can interact with your videos through comments, likes, or sharing. TikTok also allows you to restrict certain users or block them completely.
- Be Cautious with Direct Messages: Be careful about who you allow to message you. TikTok lets you filter messages from people who aren't following you, which can help prevent unwanted or spammy messages.
- Don't Click on Suspicious Links: Avoid clicking on links that seem suspicious or come from unknown sources, as they could lead to phishing scams or other harmful websites.

Security Features:
- Two-Factor Authentication: Enabling two-factor authentication (2FA) is a great way to secure your account. This adds an extra layer of security by requiring a verification code in addition to your password.
- Regularly Review Your Account Activity: Keep track of your account's activity to ensure that no unauthorized access has occurred. You can review your login activity through the settings to check for suspicious logins or activity.
- Update Your Password Regularly: Regularly change your password to keep your account secure. Use a strong, unique password that combines letters, numbers, and symbols to make it more difficult for hackers to gain access.

Real-World Example:
During a time when privacy concerns were heightened, TikTok introduced several new privacy and security features in response to feedback from users and regulatory bodies. These included enhancing options for minors' privacy, restricting messaging features for younger users, and introducing more transparent data policies.

The Boomer Bottom Line

TikTok is a fun and creative platform where users can connect, create, and engage with content. However, to ensure that TikTok remains a safe, respectful, and enjoyable environment for all, it's important to follow community guidelines, maintain respectful interactions, and prioritize privacy and security. By adhering to these principles, you can create a positive experience for both yourself and the broader TikTok community.

Chapter 14: The Psychology of TikTok Attraction

TikTok has become one of the most widely used platforms in the world, with billions of active users. While its popularity can be attributed to many factors, one of the driving forces behind its success is the psychological pull it exerts on users. It's worthwhile understanding the psychology of TikTok attraction - and even addiction - which involves looking at several cognitive and behavioral principles, from instant gratification to social validation, which encourage users to keep scrolling.

1. Instant Gratification and Dopamine
TikTok's design capitalizes on the brain's natural desire for instant gratification. As users scroll through the platform, they are consistently rewarded with new content, many times before they even finish watching the previous video. This constant stimulation creates a cycle of anticipation and reward. Each time a user watches a video, their brain releases dopamine - the "feel-good" neurotransmitter associated with pleasure and motivation. This release reinforces the behavior, encouraging them to keep scrolling for more.

Research into social media and addiction shows that platforms like TikTok, which use an algorithm to continuously present users with content tailored to their preferences, trigger the brain's reward system. This leads to an almost addictive cycle of seeking the next "hit" of dopamine.

2. The "FOMO" (Fear of Missing Out) Effect
Another psychological factor contributing to TikTok addiction is the "FOMO" effect, or the fear of missing out. TikTok's algorithm promotes viral trends, and if you're not up-to-date with the latest dances, challenges, or memes, you might feel like you're missing something important. This sense of urgency and social pressure compels users to stay engaged with the platform, even when they don't necessarily want to. The fear of missing out extends beyond trends to emotional connection. When users see their friends, favorite creators, or even celebrities engaging with TikTok, there's an implicit pressure to participate. It becomes about more than just keeping up with the trends - it becomes about staying connected to the digital world that shapes culture and social interactions.

3. Endless Scrolling: The "Variable Reward" System
TikTok's "For You" page is a classic example of a variable reward system, which is a concept used in psychology to explain addictive behavior. The idea behind a variable reward system is that users don't know what to expect next, making the experience more thrilling and captivating. This uncertainty stimulates curiosity, which, in turn, leads to compulsive behavior.

In studies on gambling addiction, for example, researchers have found that the unpredictability of rewards (such as winning at a slot machine) is what leads to an increased likelihood of addiction. TikTok uses this principle effectively, as users never know what the next video will be, yet they continue scrolling, hoping to discover something new, funny, or insightful.

4. Social Validation and the "Like" Economy

TikTok is built on a social validation model where user engagement - likes, comments, shares, and followers - becomes a measure of success. This reliance on social validation taps into the psychological principle of social comparison theory, which suggests that individuals gauge their own worth and success in comparison to others. The more likes and followers you accumulate, the more validation you receive, which strengthens your sense of belonging and self-worth.

This can create a feedback loop where users continuously post content or engage with others in order to gain validation. The desire for more followers and likes can become addictive, leading users to spend more time on the app trying to increase their visibility.

5. Escapism and the Desire for Connection

TikTok also serves as a platform for escapism. Users can lose themselves in short, engaging videos, which offer an immediate distraction from the stresses of daily life. This use of social media to escape reality is especially prominent among younger audiences, who may use TikTok as a means to cope with anxiety, stress, or feelings of loneliness.

Furthermore, TikTok provides a sense of connection that users may not find in their physical world. By watching videos, interacting with creators, or engaging in community-based challenges, users feel they are part of a larger, virtual community. This connection can become a powerful motivator to keep coming back to the app, especially for those seeking a sense of belonging.

6. The Influence of Micro-Content

One of TikTok's major innovations is its focus on micro-content. With videos typically ranging from 15 to 60 seconds, TikTok's format encourages quick consumption. These bite-sized pieces of content fit perfectly into users' limited attention spans and can be easily consumed in any environment. The brevity of each video allows users to consume large amounts of content in short bursts, further driving the cycle of addiction.

In fact, studies on media consumption suggest that shorter, easily digestible content tends to keep users hooked for longer periods, as it aligns with our brain's preference for quick rewards.

7. The Impact on Mental Health

While TikTok can be entertaining and creative, its addictive nature also comes with consequences. Excessive use can lead to feelings of isolation, anxiety, and depression, particularly if users become obsessed with gaining approval and building a social media following. The comparison with others, whether it's followers, likes, or video views, can negatively impact self-esteem and overall mental health.

Increased screen time has also been linked to disrupted sleep patterns, reduced productivity, and physical health problems such as eye strain and posture issues. It's important to strike a balance between using TikTok for enjoyment and ensuring that it doesn't interfere with other aspects of life.

The Boomer Bottom Line

The psychology of TikTok addiction revolves around various factors, from the dopamine-driven reward cycle to social validation and FOMO. Understanding these psychological mechanisms can help users recognize their behaviors and make conscious decisions about how much time they spend on the platform. Like any form of media consumption, it's essential to be mindful of the impact that excessive use can have on mental well-being, and take steps to maintain a healthy relationship with the app.

For further reading on the topic of social media addiction and the psychology behind it, you may find research articles and studies from sources such as Psychology Today and the American Psychological Association helpful.

Chapter 15: The Future of TikTok

TikTok has rapidly evolved into a global cultural powerhouse since its launch in 2016, revolutionizing how people create, share, and consume content. As the platform continues to grow and expand, many creators, marketers, and businesses are eager to understand what the future holds for TikTok. With frequent updates to its algorithm, new features, and shifts in user behavior, it's crucial to stay ahead of the curve. In this chapter, we'll explore predictions for the future of TikTok, including upcoming trends, new features, and strategies to stay relevant as the platform evolves.

1. Predictions for Trends and Features

Trend 1: Increased Integration of Augmented Reality (AR)

Augmented reality (AR) features, such as filters and effects, have already become a central part of TikTok's user experience. As the technology continues to develop, it is likely that AR will play an even bigger role in TikTok's evolution. TikTok has already begun experimenting with AR shopping experiences, where users can try on virtual items like makeup or clothes through the app. In the future, TikTok could integrate even more immersive AR features, allowing for more interactive content and experiences.

- AR Shopping and Product Integration: The growth of e-commerce on TikTok is expected to continue, with augmented reality tools allowing users to virtually try products or view them in 3D. This could lead to the further expansion of social commerce, where creators not only promote products but also allow followers to directly interact with or purchase those products through the app.
- Augmented Reality Collaborations: Look for new tools that will allow TikTok users to create more immersive videos using AR effects that blend virtual objects seamlessly into the real world. This could revolutionize creative possibilities, from dancing with virtual avatars to creating fully animated scenes.

Trend 2: Enhanced Monetization Options for Creators

TikTok has already introduced various monetization tools for creators, such as live stream gifts, the Creator Fund, and branded partnerships. In the future, we can expect these options to expand further, allowing creators to earn more revenue directly from their content.

- More Direct E-Commerce Opportunities: TikTok has been heavily investing in its e-commerce features, which are expected to evolve further. TikTok's "Shop Now" options and "TikTok Ads" are likely to become more sophisticated, allowing users to buy products seamlessly within the app.
- Creator Subscription Models: TikTok is likely to introduce subscription-based features, where fans can support their favorite creators through monthly payments. This would allow for more predictable income for creators and provide fans with exclusive content.

Trend 3: Increased Focus on Short-Form Video

The popularity of short-form content will continue to grow. TikTok's algorithm has been incredibly successful at promoting engaging, bite-sized videos, and that's not

likely to change. However, future trends may involve deeper integration with other types of short-form content that have already gained traction.
- TikTok Stories: Similar to Instagram and Facebook, TikTok Stories could become more prominent, providing users with a way to post quick updates that disappear after 24 hours. This could allow for more casual, real-time engagement with followers.
- Longer Form Content: While short-form content is TikTok's bread and butter, the platform may expand its support for longer videos. As more creators move towards producing 5-10 minute content, TikTok may adjust its algorithm to better promote longer-form content while maintaining the platform's appeal to those who prefer quick entertainment.

Trend 4: AI and Machine Learning Integration
TikTok's algorithm is already known for its highly personalized feed, but the platform is likely to push the boundaries of machine learning even further. AI could be used to refine content recommendations, making it easier for creators to reach the right audience and improve user engagement.
- AI-Driven Content Creation: TikTok may offer new tools for automated content creation, allowing creators to generate videos using AI tools that suggest ideas based on trends and user preferences.
- Better Personalization: As TikTok refines its machine learning algorithms, users may see an even more customized feed, with videos catered not only to their interests but also based on their behavior, time of day, and even the emotional tone of the content.

2. How to Stay Ahead as TikTok Evolves

Stay Informed About New Features and Tools
TikTok frequently rolls out new features, tools, and updates to improve user experience. As a creator, staying on top of these changes is essential. Whenever a new feature is announced, take the time to understand how it works and how it can benefit your content strategy.
- Participate in Beta Tests: TikTok often offers early access to certain features through beta programs. By joining these programs, you'll be able to experiment with new tools before they're made available to the public, giving you a head start.
- Join TikTok Creator Communities: Many creators share tips, tricks, and updates in private Facebook groups or on Reddit. By participating in these communities, you'll stay updated on the latest platform developments.

Experiment with New Content Formats
As trends evolve, so too must your content. TikTok thrives on creative experimentation, so you should aim to stay flexible and willing to try new formats as they emerge.
- Leverage New Effects and Filters: TikTok regularly introduces new AR filters, effects, and editing tools. Keep an eye on these updates and be quick to adopt them to stay relevant. Using the latest effects will keep your content fresh and engaging.

- Stay on Top of Hashtags: Hashtags often evolve to reflect current events, trends, or challenges. Pay attention to trending hashtags and incorporate them into your videos to increase visibility.

Create Content That is Adaptable Across Platforms
As TikTok evolves, it is also integrating more closely with other social media platforms. Cross-promotion across Instagram, YouTube, and other networks is essential for expanding your audience.
- Use TikTok's Share Features: TikTok makes it easy to share your videos directly to Instagram, Twitter, or Facebook. Use this functionality to drive traffic between your accounts and gain exposure to a larger audience.
- Diversify Your Content Across Platforms: While TikTok is your primary platform, don't forget to maintain a presence on other networks. Platforms like Instagram and YouTube provide opportunities for more in-depth content, which can be cross-promoted on TikTok.

Engage with Your Audience
Even as TikTok evolves, one thing will always remain constant: the need for creators to engage with their followers. Building a strong community and interacting with viewers will be just as important in the future as it is today.
- Use TikTok's Live Streaming Feature: Going live allows you to engage with your followers in real-time. This personal connection can help you build a more loyal fanbase.
- Respond to Comments and DMs: Always take the time to engage with your followers by responding to comments or direct messages. This helps create a sense of community and shows your followers that you value their input.

The Boomer Bottom Line
The future of TikTok is bright and full of exciting possibilities. By staying informed about new trends, exploring emerging features, and being adaptable to changes in the platform, you can position yourself for success in the ever-evolving TikTok landscape. Whether it's experimenting with new content formats, leveraging advanced features, or simply maintaining a strong connection with your audience, staying ahead of the curve will ensure you remain a relevant and successful creator for years to come.
As TikTok continues to evolve, remember that the core of the platform is creativity, authenticity, and engagement. Keep these values at the heart of your content strategy, and you'll be ready for whatever changes the future brings.

Chapter 16: Revisiting Viral Videos and Suggestions

What Makes a Video Go Viral on TikTok?
TikTok's algorithm is highly sophisticated, and understanding why certain videos go viral can provide valuable insight into what works on the platform. While there's no guaranteed formula for virality, certain patterns and characteristics are often present in the most successful videos. From humorous skits and clever edits to inspiring dance routines and heartfelt moments, viral videos tap into universal emotions like laughter, surprise, or awe.

In this chapter, we will break down examples of viral videos on TikTok, explain why they were successful, and provide suggestions for how you can create your own viral-worthy content.

Understanding Viral Video Elements
Before diving into specific examples, let's take a look at some of the common elements that make TikTok videos go viral:

1. Relatability
Videos that are relatable tend to strike a chord with audiences, making them more likely to share and engage with the content. Whether it's a funny moment from everyday life, a commentary on a current trend, or a personal anecdote, content that resonates with viewers on a personal level often has the potential to go viral.

2. Trend Participation
TikTok thrives on trends, whether it's a dance challenge, viral sound, or popular hashtag. Videos that successfully tap into these trends often benefit from increased visibility because TikTok's algorithm promotes trending content to a broader audience.

3. Emotional Appeal
Videos that evoke strong emotions, such as laughter, awe, or empathy, are more likely to be shared. Emotionally charged content, whether funny or touching, tends to perform well because it prompts viewers to engage with the video.

4. Catchy Music and Sounds
TikTok's integration of music is key to many viral videos. A catchy sound or song often propels a video to viral status. Many successful videos have become viral because of the clever use of audio tracks or sounds that align perfectly with the visuals.

5. Unique Editing or Creativity
Creative edits or unique video structures can make a video stand out in a crowded feed. High-quality production, clever transitions, or unexpected twists add intrigue, making people want to watch and share.

Ten Viral TikTok Videos (and Why They Went Viral)
Here are ten examples of videos that garnered massive attention on TikTok. These examples highlight different types of content, demonstrating that virality can come from humor, creativity, or simply being in the right place at the right time.

1. Charli D'Amelio – The Renegade Dance (2019)
Charli D'Amelio's viral dance video to the song "Lottery" became one of TikTok's

most iconic moments. The viral nature of this video is a perfect example of how dance challenges can drive massive engagement. Charli's impeccable timing and ability to match the rhythm of the music with precise choreography made her video a must-watch.

Key Takeaway: Participate in trending challenges, and execute them with precision. Charli's success is a result of not only following a trend but mastering it.

2. Nathan Apodaca – "Dreams" Longboarding Video (2020)

Nathan Apodaca went viral after posting a video of himself skateboarding while drinking cranberry juice and lip-syncing to Fleetwood Mac's "Dreams." This spontaneous, carefree moment resonated with millions because of its laid-back, positive energy. It also tapped into the nostalgia of Fleetwood Mac, appealing to a wide audience.

Key Takeaway: Authenticity and fun moments can lead to virality, especially when paired with the right soundtrack. Sometimes, it's not about perfection - just capturing a genuine moment.

3. Bella Poarch – "Savage Love" Lip Sync (2020)

Bella Poarch's lip-syncing video to the song "Savage Love" featured a simple, yet incredibly engaging visual: her smiling and making minimal gestures while she mouthed the lyrics. The simplicity, combined with an infectious tune and Bella's charm, helped make the video one of the most-liked TikToks ever.

Key Takeaway: Sometimes simplicity is key. Create content that is easy to follow and entertaining, and don't underestimate the power of a catchy song.

4. TikTok's #SeaShanty Trend (2021)

The viral sea shanty trend took over TikTok in early 2021. Users across the globe joined in on creating and remixing sea shanty songs, using the popular hashtag #SeaShanty. The trend gained traction because of its collaborative nature, bringing together creators with diverse talents.

Key Takeaway: Trends that encourage collaboration and creativity across the community can lead to explosive virality. Create content that encourages others to participate, and your video might just go viral.

5. "WAP" Dance Challenge (2020)

When Cardi B and Megan Thee Stallion's song "WAP" was released, it quickly became a TikTok sensation. The accompanying dance challenge brought out thousands of viral videos, showcasing the creativity of the TikTok dance community. People of all ages participated, adding their twist to the routine.

Key Takeaway: Popular music can drive virality, especially if paired with a well-executed dance challenge. Be prepared to jump on trends early for the best chance of going viral.

6. The "Flip the Switch" Challenge (2020)

This viral challenge involved two people standing in front of a mirror while the song "Nonstop" by Drake played. At the moment the lyrics said "Flip the switch," the two participants would switch positions, often with comedic results. The trend was widely popular and generated countless variations across TikTok.

Key Takeaway: Participating in viral challenges is a great way to increase your exposure. Adding a unique spin to a well-known trend can help make your video stand out.

7. @ltsjojosiwa – Dance Videos and Transitions (2020)
Jojo Siwa's transformation on TikTok, including her dance moves and creative transitions, captivated viewers. Her ability to seamlessly transition from one look or dance to another created an immersive experience that had people hitting the share button.
Key Takeaway: Mastering video transitions and adding visually engaging elements can make your content more shareable. Creativity and polish go a long way on TikTok.

8. Dog in a Hot Dog Costume (2020)
In a simpler example, a video of a dog dressed as a hot dog while walking around went viral purely because of its adorable, heartwarming nature. Sometimes, cute animals and unexpected moments are all it takes to create viral content.
Key Takeaway: Sometimes the unexpected, like a cute dog in a funny costume, can deliver viral success. Play into what people find entertaining or heartwarming.

9. @Chrisudalla – Rube Goldberg Machine (2020)
Chris Udalla became famous for his intricate Rube Goldberg machines made from household items. These creative, physics-based contraptions garnered millions of views because of their complexity and novelty.
Key Takeaway: If you have a talent for creativity or building something unique, it can be the key to going viral. Don't be afraid to show off your skill set in fun, engaging ways.

10. @Doggosdoingthings – Compilation Videos (2020)
Doggosdoingthings is a TikTok account that simply shares hilarious videos of dogs doing funny things. This niche account grew quickly due to the universal love for pets and animals, with users sharing the content widely.
Key Takeaway: Niche content, especially if it involves pets or relatable humor, can perform well. If you find a specific angle that resonates with people, you can build a dedicated following.

How to Create Your Own Viral TikTok Video
After looking at these examples, here are a few practical tips to help you create your own viral video:
1. Participate in Trends Early: The earlier you hop on a trend, the more likely it is that your video will gain traction. Follow trending sounds and challenges closely.
2. Keep It Short and Engaging: Attention spans are short on TikTok. Aim to keep your videos under 30 seconds and hook viewers in the first few seconds.
3. Use Popular Music: Leverage TikTok's music library to choose trending songs or sounds that align with your content. Music plays a big role in TikTok's viral culture.
4. Add Humor or Surprise: Whether through unexpected twists or funny commentary, humor often drives shares. People like to be surprised or entertained.

5. Create Emotional Connections: Content that evokes a strong emotional reaction (laughter, empathy, awe) is more likely to be shared, helping you reach a wider audience.
6. Engage with Your Audience: Respond to comments and create content that invites engagement. The more interaction your video gets, the more likely it is to be pushed by the TikTok algorithm.

The Boomer Bottom Line

By understanding the elements that contribute to virality and studying successful examples, you can apply these strategies to your own TikTok content. While there's no guaranteed way to go viral, staying consistent, engaging with your audience, and creating unique, high-quality content will help increase your chances. Tap into trends, get creative, and, above all, have fun with the process!

Chapter 17: Embrace Your TikTok Journey

As you embark on your TikTok journey, it's important to remember that success on the platform doesn't happen overnight. Whether you're aiming to build a personal brand, promote a business, or simply express yourself creatively, TikTok offers an unparalleled opportunity to connect with a vast, diverse global audience. However, like any journey, it requires dedication, experimentation, and a willingness to learn from both successes and setbacks.

This final chapter offers encouragement as you move forward, highlights key takeaways from the book, and shares where you can find ongoing support and inspiration to keep you motivated.

Encouragement and Motivation for Your TikTok Journey

TikTok can be intimidating at first. With its complex algorithm, fast-moving trends, and ever-changing features, it might feel like you're stepping into a whirlwind. But the beauty of TikTok lies in its democratization of content creation - anyone, regardless of their background or experience, can go viral if they produce engaging, authentic content.

Remember: Consistency is Key Success on TikTok, just like any social media platform, is built on consistency. Uploading videos regularly will help you stay top-of-mind for your audience, and more importantly, it allows you to keep refining your content and style. Whether you post once a day, three times a week, or bi-weekly, stick to a schedule that works for you and your audience.

Embrace Creativity and Authenticity One of TikTok's greatest strengths is its ability to showcase raw, unpolished creativity. While it's easy to get caught up in what others are doing, the most successful TikTokers often stand out because they stay true to their own voice. Don't be afraid to take risks with your content, try out new trends, or even create your own. The more authentic and genuine your content feels, the more likely your audience will connect with it.

Failure is Part of the Process Not every video you create will be a hit, and that's okay! TikTok's algorithm is unpredictable, and even the most seasoned creators experience dips in engagement. Use these moments to learn and adapt. Maybe it's time to try a new content format, explore different music, or dive deeper into niche topics that resonate with your followers. Every "failure" is an opportunity to grow.

Summary of Key Takeaways

- Master the Basics: Knowing how to use TikTok's features, such as creating and editing videos, using effects and filters, and adding music, is essential. Familiarity with the platform's interface will help you navigate its features with ease.
- Consistency and Scheduling: Successful TikTokers post regularly, whether that's daily, weekly, or bi-weekly. Find a rhythm that works for you and stick with it.
- Engage with Your Audience: TikTok thrives on interaction. Respond to comments, engage with your followers' content, and take part in challenges and trends to keep your audience engaged.
- Stay Current with Trends: TikTok is constantly evolving, and staying up-to-date with trends, sounds, and viral challenges is crucial to gaining exposure. Participating in trends allows you to be part of the larger TikTok conversation.

- Leverage Analytics: TikTok's built-in analytics tool is a powerful resource to help you understand your audience and performance. Use this data to refine your content strategy and focus on what works.
- Experiment and Take Risks: Don't be afraid to step outside your comfort zone. The most engaging TikTok videos are often the ones that take risks, whether that's through new creative formats, humor, or unexpected content.
- Prioritize Safety and Etiquette: Always follow TikTok's community guidelines, and be respectful toward others. Negative comments and trolls can be a part of the experience, but remember to maintain a positive and professional attitude online.

Where to Find Ongoing Support and Inspiration

While this book has provided you with the tools and strategies to succeed on TikTok, the journey doesn't end here. Fortunately, there are plenty of resources to keep you inspired, informed, and connected with other TikTokers.
- TikTok Creators' Hub: The official TikTok Creators' Hub is a fantastic place to access resources, tips, and success stories from experienced creators. TikTok frequently offers advice on how to use the platform effectively and make the most of its features.
- Online Communities: Facebook groups, Reddit threads, and Twitter spaces are full of TikTok creators and enthusiasts who are eager to share their experiences and knowledge. Joining these communities will keep you informed about the latest trends and provide a supportive space for asking questions and sharing your progress.
- TikTok Influencer and Creator Courses: Many creators have launched online courses designed to help others grow on TikTok. These courses can offer deep dives into topics such as monetization, viral strategies, and content creation. Look for reputable influencers or marketers offering educational resources.
- Follow Fellow Creators: Don't just watch TikTok for inspiration - engage with other creators. Many successful TikTokers share their experiences, tips, and behind-the-scenes processes. Watching how others evolve on the platform can give you ideas and motivation for your own content.
- Stay Updated on TikTok's Blog: TikTok's official blog regularly shares new features, updates, and insights from the platform's development team. It's an excellent resource for staying on top of changes and understanding how they affect your content strategy.

Final Thoughts

Okay boomer, you now have the knowledge and strategies to embark on your TikTok journey with confidence. Whether you're creating for fun, building a brand, or hoping to go viral, the most important thing is to stay authentic, stay consistent, and continue experimenting. TikTok's dynamic nature means that there's always something new to learn, and as long as you stay curious and flexible, you'll be able to navigate whatever comes next.

Remember, every TikTok creator started somewhere - and many of the biggest names on the platform began with nothing more than a passion for creating and a willingness to learn. Your journey has just begun, and the possibilities are endless. Don't be afraid to take risks, learn from your experiences, and enjoy the process of expressing yourself on one of the world's most exciting social platforms.

There's nothing stopping you! The app will most certainly deliver your video to viewers, so grab their attention and you'll be on your way. Go ahead - take the leap, create, and share your unique voice with the world!

www.ingramcontent.com/pod-product-compliance
Lightning Source LLC
Chambersburg PA
CBHW071111240526
45469CB00006BD/2437